An Easy to Understand Beginner's Guide to Investing

By Jayson C. Flores

An Easy to Understand Beginner's Guide to Investing
Jayson C. Flores

Copyright © 2016 Jayson C. Flores

All rights reserved. This book or any portion thereof may not be reproduced without the written permission of the author except for use of brief quotations in a book review.

Disclaimer: The materials presented in this book are for educational purposes only. They do not in any way constitute any professional or expert advice for any particular person or persons. The sale of this book comes with an understanding that the author does not render professional or expert advice. The reader has the sole responsibility for his or her actions. The author in no way guarantee any result that may be obtained from using the contents of this book. The author specifically disclaims any and all liabilities, losses, direct or indirect, that result from the application or use of any of the content of this book. While effort has been made to ensure that the information presented in this book is accurate, the author makes no warranties or representation on the completeness or accuracy of the content of this book. This book contains information from sources the author believes to be accurate and reliable. However, because of the possibility of human or mechanical error as well as other factors, all information contained herein is provided on an "AS IS" basis without any guarantee. The author specifically disclaims all warranties, including but not limited to warranties of suitability for a specific purpose. The author assumes no responsibility for any contrary or differing interpretation of the topics presented herein. Any semblance of any person or organization is purely coincidental and totally unintentional.

Under no circumstances should any material found in this book be construed as an offering of securities or of investment advice. Should the reader require investment advice or any other expert or professional advice, he/she should seek a professional investment advisor or a professional or expert in that particular field.

To Financial Freedom

Table of Content

The Time Machine: Show Me My Future 7

Not Saving Money is a Good Thing 15

Unlike What You May have Been Taught: The Secret to Accumulating Wealth is NOT Investing..............................21

Robbing a Bank is Becoming More an Option 25

I Would Like to Invest in Your Meal 29

I Want a Piece of Your Pie 34

Uncertain vs. Less Uncertain Investments 38

As Safe as it Gets Type of Investment 45

The Thief..49

An Emotional Investment..60

I Have the Money, Where Should I Put It...............................65

A Tailor Fit Investment Portfolio 74

Diversification 76

Captain of the Ship Investor...82

Autopilot Investing 92

Epilogue...101

Important Reminder to a Beginning Investor.......................102

Expanding Your Investment Portfolio 103

Investments Reserved for the Rich 106

Here is What to Do When You are Not Yet Rich and Financially Sophisticated 109

The Time Machine: Show Me My Future

Technology is getting better and better and it keeps surprising us with innovative products that change how we live.

Suppose one day while you were surfing the internet your eyes were suddenly drawn to a search engine result that says "Virtual Time Machine". You clicked on the link and it brings you to a website that claims that they have VR goggles that can show you your future (but only up to two months into the future). You were very skeptic but somewhat amazed at the same time thinking that people actually post these obvious "scams" online. You thought, maybe there are suckers out there that fall for these outrageous things. You were ready to click on the close tab button, but the thought of "What if this was true? It is not like they are claiming to see many years into the future. If it's true, it could be fun. And it only cost $30." The shop was just a 15-minute drive from your apartment and an even shorter 10-minute drive from your place of work. The thought of a bargain made you decide to click on the button that says "Request for an appointment". You chose this coming Thursday to visit the shop.

Days before your appointment, you find yourself excited and constantly thinking of your 'time machine' appointment. Finally, the day came. After clocking out from work you got into your 6-year old car and drove to the shop. You arrived at the shop. It was an average looking shop in a somewhat obscure neighborhood. You entered the shop and a guy in his early 30s greeted you. He was wearing a regular gray shirt, jeans, rubber shoes and eyeglasses with thick black frame. The thought of a scam keeps popping in your mind. But it was subtle. The guy showed you to the room at the back. There, an old person, who looks like a grandpa with fuzzy hair, wearing a white lab coat smiled at you and points to a chair in the middle of the room. You walked towards the chair and sat down feeling a little anxious now. The old guy handed you a pair of VR goggles, without uttering a single word. It was a regular looking VR goggles except that the wire from the goggles leads to a box where hundreds of wires are attached and those wires lead to 4 big cabinet-like super processors of some kind. Now you are feeling really anxious and almost felt like you are a guinea pig in an experiment. You wanted to ask for some legal papers in case this experience harms your brain or your body in anyway, but the guys are charging just $30. There is no way that it would be a legal battle worth fighting, just in case. So you nervously but willingly put on the goggles.

The screen was still dark. You felt your index finger was slipped into a clip-like sensor (something like what they use to monitor someone's heartbeat). It was the younger guy who did that and said that it was necessary to map your fingerprint for the machine to project your future.

"Are you ready to see your future?" the old guy said with a foreign sounding accent.

Thinking there is no turning back now, you said "Yes."

The screen lit up, hazy at first, but then it became clearer and you see yourself standing in an airport. But not an airport you have been to. The glass walls of the airport reveal tropical looking scenery. You look for any sort of signage that tells you where you are. It was not long before your saw one. You are in an airport in Hawaii!

The younger guy said he will put the VR glove on your left hand. He said that it would allow you to choose from the menu in the VR screen. You said okay.

The menu function allows you to fast forward in time or reverse in time. You chose to fast forward 3 days from when you were at the airport and it shows you a scene that you are on a romantic date.

Dinner on the sand, by the beach, with torches that add to the romantic atmosphere scattered around the restaurant.

For thirty minutes you toyed with the VR goggles. Then, when you chose to move forward 1 year from when you were at the airport the screen showed "PREMIUM SUBSCRIPTION REQUIRED".

You took off the goggles and you see in front of you the older guy and younger guy both smiling at you. They knew you enjoyed the experience.

You narrated to them that 1 week prior to coming to the shop you had already booked a flight and hotel for your vacation in Hawaii. It will be your first time there. For you, that verifies that this VR time machine really works.

Wanting to see further into the future, you asked how you can get a premium subscription. The older guy said that the service is not yet available as the software is still in its final stages of refinement. The younger guy interrupted the older guy and said that what the older guy meant is that the images that are projected into the VR goggles won't be as vivid. It may appear like a black and white movie. Generating images several years or decades into the future is harder to do than a 2-month projection, he continued. And there could be glitches, he added. You said "No problem," excited of what the future holds.

They made you fill up a questionnaire on their computer. They said that your answers will aid the algorithm to project a more accurate future. After finishing the questionnaire and after uploading a different software into their computer they hooked you up again.

The image is in black and white, like what they said. You are in a house, a good sized home, simple yet elegant (your taste). You suspect that you own the house. You always wanted to get out of your small apartment and buy a house with a big yard. Judging from the looks of the house it is made for a millionaire.

"Could it be that I will become a millionaire?" the thought excites you. In your mind you are asking if you were promoted several times in the past for you to be able to afford such a home. You chose in the VR menu to go to a certain location. You chose "Bank". The software brings you to the day when you visited the bank. Posted at the bank wall was the date that day. You recognize that you were 33 years into the future (i.e. 33 years since you started working). At the bank you are excited to see how big your account is. You were almost certain that it would be big based on the house you have seen so far. When you looked at your account it was considerably small. Certainly not the kind you would expect of a rich person. It was depressingly small, even for your current income level. Depressed about the amount in the bank account and confused by the size and elegance of the house, you accessed the VR menu and wanted to move 3 more years into the future. You are now panicking that you have gone broke and that you would soon lose the house. Before even pressing the button on the VR menu, the screen went dark.

The younger guy immediately took off the goggles from you. You were sweating. You whispered "I'm broke". The older guy said that there was a glitch, like what they said, and that the system showed you an alternate future. "Really?" you said feeling a little relieved (relieved from the thought that you won't have money in the future). Still panic stricken, you failed to notice the gentleman (who looked like in his early 40s) wearing a nice suit and looks like a client as well.

"You look terrible," he said to you.

"I saw my future. I'm broke. My bank account is close to nothing," you replied.

"What else did you see?" the gentleman asked.

"I have an elegant house," you said.

"That seems normal to me," he replied as though he was so sure of his answer.

You were baffled by his response. "Normal?" you politely said to him.

"Yes. Most millionaires don't put their money in banks. They only put some in.", he replied.

"The name is William. I'm an investor," he introduced himself.

"You mean like stocks and bonds?" you said.

You were about to say more but the older guy interrupted and said that they may have found the glitch. The older guy asked if you answered in the questionnaire that you like and know investments. "No. I save my money in the bank. That's what I like to do. It is safe there," you replied.

"The glitch in the software showed you an alternate future in which you did not like to save money in the bank but invested it instead", the older guy said in his foreign-sounding accent.

After hearing that, you uttered "William, can you help me get started on investing?"

William, as if expecting you would say that said "Meet me tomorrow morning for coffee. We can have a brief chat."

Not Saving Money is a Good Thing

At the coffee shop

"I like starting my day with a cup of coffee in this place. It's relaxing. I like to watch…"

"William, why don't millionaires trust banks?" you interjected as you were eager to know more.

"What do you mean?" he said and you replied that he mentioned that millionaires don't put much money in the bank.

"It is not that millionaires don't trust banks, it is just that banks are the last place they would want to put their money. Money is not safe there."

People save rather than invest primarily because of 3 reasons or some combination of those reasons: (1) they feel that money is safe in the bank (later you will see this not to be true) or (2) they have heard of people who lost money in investments or (3) they want to invest but are overwhelmed by its perceived complexities (much like a grandparent trying to learn using a smartphone), so saving is really just the way to go.

Let us compare saving to investing:

Let's say you left $2,000 in your personal savings account in your favorite bank for 30 years and that your alternate self (the one projected by the VR Time Machine) puts $2,000 dollars in the stock market and also left it there for 30 years.

Here's what happens to $2,000 in 30 years:

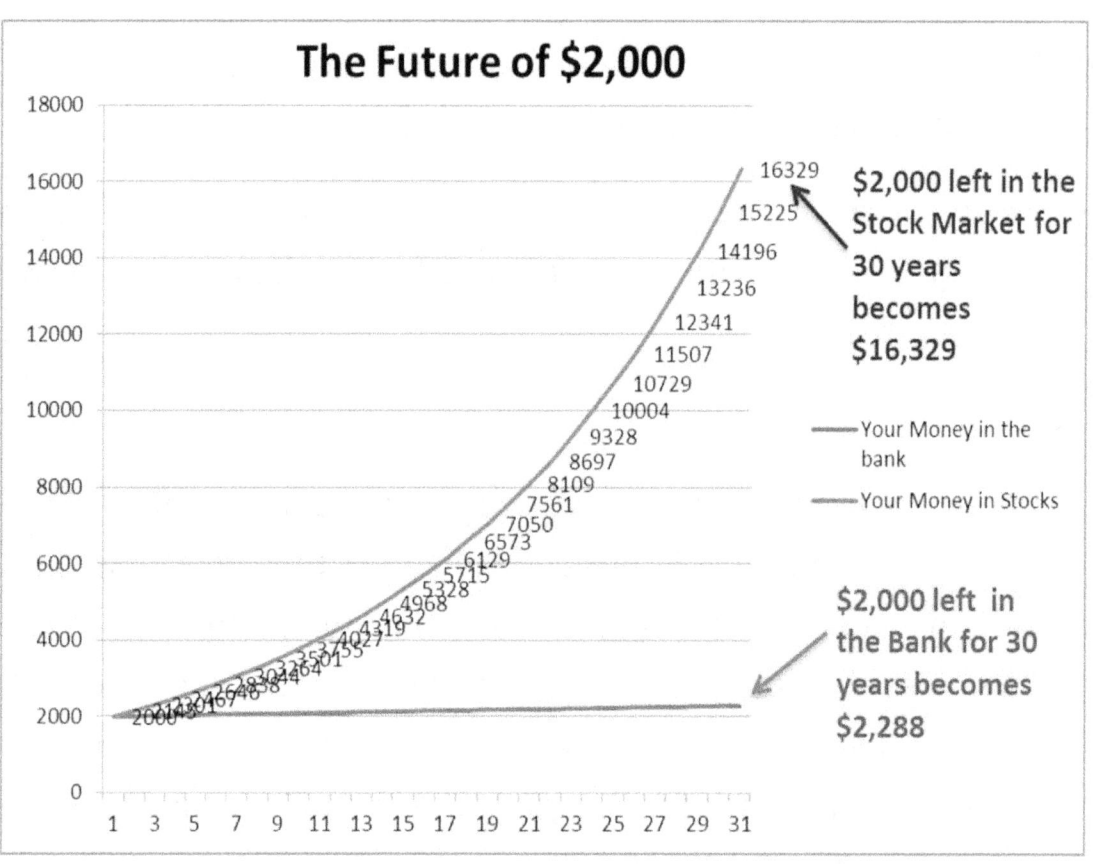

Data used: US deposit interest rate 0.452% (average 2006-2015), stock market return 7.5% (S&P 500 average return 2006-2015)

Now you can clearly see the difference between investing and saving—your $2,288 vs. your VR self's whopping $16,329! You put in the same amount, but your VR self ends up with **7x** more money (with these level of returns, becoming a millionaire does not seem so far-fetched after all).

Even if your VR self had only left $1,000 in the stock market, your VR self still beats you and end up with **3.6x** the money you have, even as your VR self invested half the money you put in (see graph below).

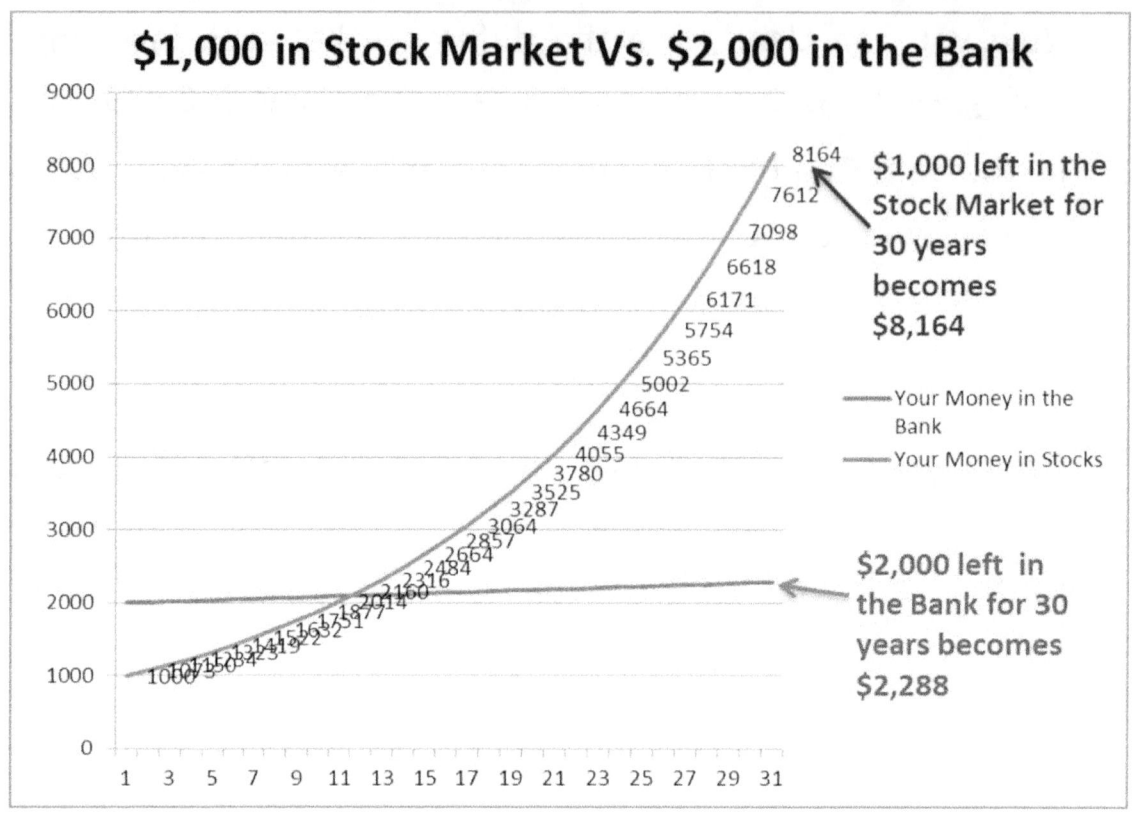

Data used: US deposit interest rate 0.452% (average 2006-2015), stock market return 7.5% (S&P 500 average return 2006-2015)

Your VR self starts overtaking you by end of year 11 (you have $2,101 and your VR self has $2,160). You have been ahead for about 11 years. But at the start of year 12, your VR self starts to really pull away because of the spectacular returns from the investment.

"You see, banks are for holding money, *not* for growing money. Investments are for growing money. And if you do not invest, you won't be able to live an alternate life of comfort at the very least," William said

There are places where you can put your money other than in a savings account. We will focus on the major and most popular asset classes.

You can put your money in:

1. the stock market
2. bonds
3. Treasury Bills (T-Bills)

I will explain each of them later. There are more investment vehicles out there. But these are the primary asset classes and that as a beginning investor you should start with them. You can always explore other investment vehicles in the future, when you have gained more experience investing.

"I think you should finish your coffee and rush to work. We can have a brief chat again tomorrow over coffee," William said as he put on the table his black laptop.

Unlike What You May have Been Taught: The Secret to Accumulating Wealth is NOT Investing

Your VR self is able to accumulate more money because of a friend. It's not necessarily William the investor (although he might have been the one who taught your VR self how to invest).

At the coffee shop

"Coffee for two please," William said to the attendant.

"How can a simple person make it big and accumulate wealth?" William asked you.

"Rob a bank?" you jokingly said.

"NO," he replied.

"Two banks?" you quickly retorted.

Let's say you have spare cash of $2,000 and you have decided to invest that cash. You can do one of two things (described below):

1. A $2,000 investment earning 10% interest for 40 years will give you $8,000 if you withdraw the $200 yearly interest ($2,000 x 0.10) every year.

2. The same $2,000 investment earning the same interest of 10% for 40 years, but this time you don't withdraw any of the interest for the whole 40 years—will give you $90,519.

$90,519 is 11.3x bigger than $8,000

Not withdrawing the interest is essentially reinvesting. That means you are essentially putting back in the interest that your money has gained to earn more interest. And that is what gives you the spectacular returns. Compound interest (or compounding) makes you earn interest from interest. It is like a snow ball that you roll down the hill, which picks up more and more snow as it rolls down. Visually your money growth looks like this as time passes(see next page):

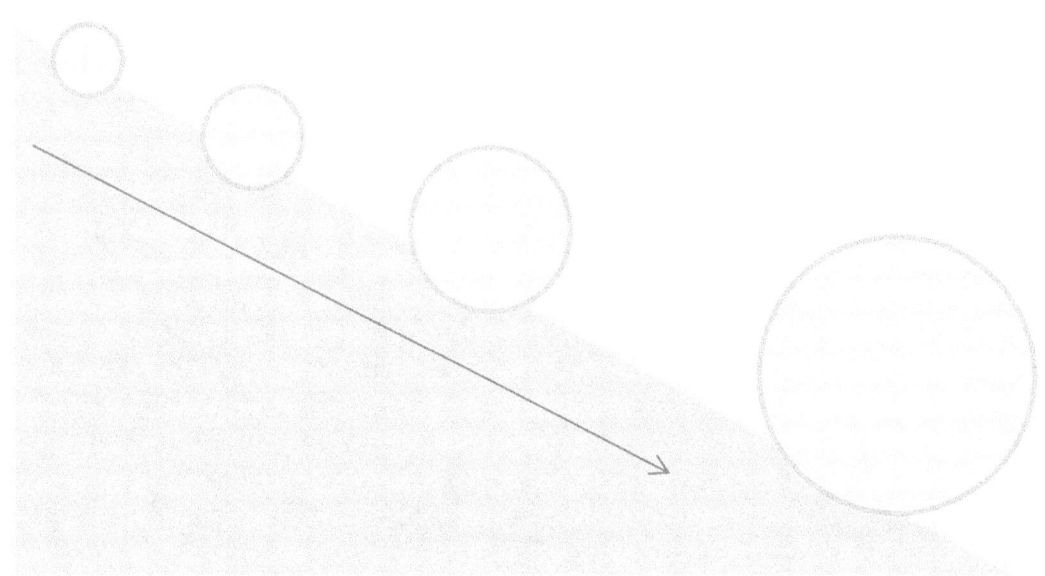

It starts out small when it begins to roll down, but towards the latter part, you will be amazed at how it has gotten so big. Compound interest can do that. That is why it is called the 8th wonder of the world.

In chart form, your money growth looks like this:

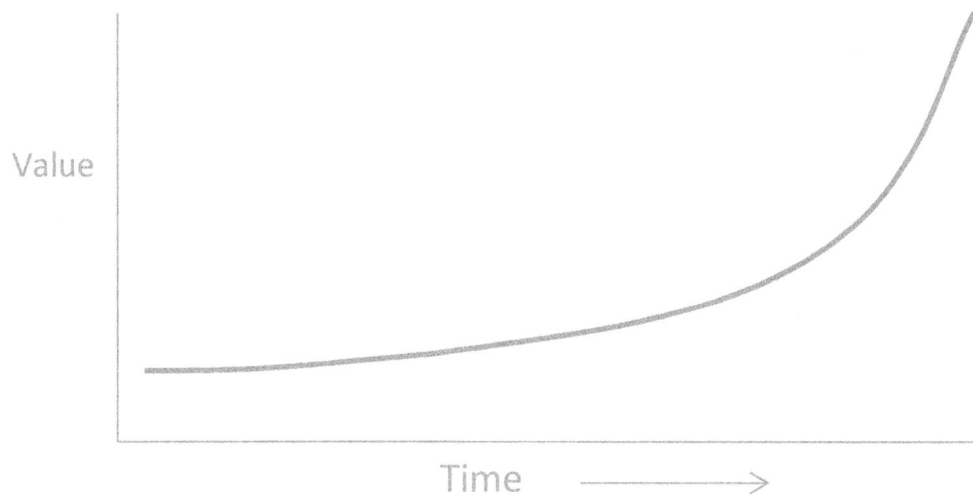

"The key to accumulating wealth is not investing. It is *re*-investing to get that snowball effect, to benefit from compounding or compound interest," William uttered.

"I see. Investing is not enough. Well, I have to go. There is this deadline I need to meet. I will meet you here again tomorrow," you said to William.

William nodded as he brings out his black laptop.

Robbing a Bank is Becoming More an Option

At the coffee shop the next morning

"To your credit, robbing a bank (or two) is what we need to do. But we make sure the police is not on our tail," William said.

"You did know I was only kidding," you replied.

To explain:

Let's have two persons with the following descriptions

Bob	Martha
Employee at a local pharmacy	Owns a pizza parlor
Has extra cash	Needs cash to buy a second oven for expansion

Bob and Martha, recognizing that they are in a situation where they can both benefit decided to make a deal.

The transaction:

Bob	Martha
Decides he will not spend his money now (he will spend his money in the future) and lends the money to Martha	Takes the money and spends it on a second oven

Sometime in the future:

Martha	Bob
Having made more money from selling pizza cooked in her new oven, returns Bob's money plus a little extra (the interest)	Takes his money plus interest and spends it

The outcome:

Martha	Bob
has a second oven from which she makes more pizza to earn more money	Receives more money than he originally put in

This is a happy ending for both.

"I have to hand it to you. Their deal is essentially like a bank transaction. Only this time it is Bob who profited not the bank. The bank has essentially been robbed. At least that is one way of looking at it. But the truth is Bob fairly competed with the bank's business, so it is perfectly legal," William explained.

And that is how investments work. Those who have cash today will defer their spending to a future date in return for some extra cash. Those who require money receives the cash from investors (like Bob or you) and spend it today. And then, at a future date, repay the amount borrowed plus interest.

"If you do as Bob consistently but you don't spend the extra cash that you earned but rather reinvest it, that extra cash is going to become bigger and bigger. And that is what will make you rich," William further explained to you.

"Meet me for lunch. I have more to tell you," said William.

"That's great. See you later then."

The transaction is essentially lending money to earn interest. Another investment is ownership or part-ownership of a business. This type of investment will be explained later.

Next, we will take a look at the major asset classes and their characteristics.

I Would Like to Invest in Your Meal

Lunch at a restaurant

"William, I often hear bonds in business news. I hear people make money from it but I don't know what it exactly means nor do I understand it. But when I hear it, it sounds like a commitment to me," you said to William.

"Bonds sound like a technical term and yes, people do make money from them. Bonds are actually simple," William replied.

To explain:

Let's say you and your co-worker had lunch out in a nearby restaurant. After the meal, when your co-worker was about to pay for his meal and reached in for his wallet, he was shocked, because he had left his wallet in the office. You are sitting next to him and he asked you if you can lend him $15. Being a good friend, you lent him the $15 and then he handed you a napkin, and written on the napkin is "IOU $15 plus 25 cents interest, thanks pal." Your co-worker just issued a bond. A bond is an IOU. It is a promise to pay you back the amount plus interest. You essentially invested in your co-worker's bond. Bonds are essentially debt obligations.

"I knew bonds were a commitment," you muttered.

Another example:

Let's say the government needs money to fund a new railway project. The government can borrow money from people who have extra cash. In other words, the government will issue a bond. Let's say you purchased a $1,000 10-year government bond. Written on the bond is: "The holder of this security will receive $20 yearly for 10 years and on the 10th year the holder will receive the principal of $1,000". Buying the bond entitles you to receive a total of $1,200 ($20 x 10 years plus the $1,000 principal) as payment for letting the government use your money for 10 years.

The way a bond works is that it pays out only the interest (called coupons) in the years prior to the maturity date and on the last year, at the maturity date, they will pay out the last coupon and principal as well. The way a bond works is different when compared to a person who takes out a 2-year $24,000-loan from a bank, in which case the borrower repays the bank a monthly installment of $1,000 plus interest for 24 months. In this case the person pays the interest and a portion of the principal on a monthly basis. To reiterate, in a bond coupons are paid out first and the principal is paid out at maturity (maturity means at the end of the term of the bond).

Now for Corporate Bonds:

Corporate bonds are the same as government bonds, except that they are issued by companies or corporations.

For example, a company that makes cars may need to upgrade the robots they are using to paint their cars. They can issue corporate bonds and use the proceeds from the sale of the bond to fund the robot upgrade. And just like government bonds, they will pay out only the coupons in the early years and on the last year the last coupon and the principal.

Bonds have maturities. Some have short-term, others medium-term and long-term. Maturity simply means the length of time it takes before you receive the principal. Thus with a 10-year $1000-

bond, you will receive the $1000 principal after 10 years. These will be explained more in a later section.

"Let me see if I got this right, William. If I have $10,000, I will defer spending it. Instead I will use it to buy, let's say ten $1000 2-year bonds which pays 10% coupon. In those 2 years I will be receiving a total of $2000 dollars in coupon payments (interest). I will not spend any of the $2000. I will add that to the $10,000 I will get back at maturity date of the bond. By the end of 2 years, I will have a total of $12,000 which I can use to buy, this time, not just ten but twelve $1000 2-year bonds. Then I do this over and over. And let's say after 30 years of doing this my "seed" money which is $10,000 becomes…"

"$174,494. That is more that 17x your seed money," William interjected.

"You can also look at it this way: have you not invested and just spent your $10,000 dollars, you won't have $174,494 in the future," William added.

"Now, is it getting clearer why your VR self is able to afford the elegant home that you saw?" William asked.

"So far you have opened my eyes to new possibilities, William. For that, let me treat you pizza tomorrow, dinner time," you said to William with a thankful heart.

I Want a Piece of Your Pie

At the pizza place

"The pizza here is awesome, William. You know, I never wanted to have a job. What I want is to put up my own business but I don't have that big amount of money to do it yet."

"You can own stocks," William said.

To explain what a stock is:

Think of Martha's Pizza Parlor and let's suppose that it is one of the most successful pizza parlor in town, and let's say that you also have $40,000 in spare cash, and that you can say to Martha "Here's my $40,000. Take it. I would like to be your business partner". Let's say Martha agreed, takes your money and puts it into good use. After a year, the pizza parlor made $200,000 in profits. As a business partner, you will get your fair share of the profits.

That is a stock. It is part-ownership of a business. When you invest your money into a business you will get your fair share of the profits. However, you will also take a hit if the business loses money instead. That's part of the risk of being a business owner. You don't know for sure what kind of a return you will get from your investment. It varies. But it has the potential to give you a far better return had you just lent your money to Martha in order to receive a small interest on it. A part-owner of a business, in this case, is also called a stockholder or shareholder.

As a stockholder you do not necessarily get involved in the operation of the business. Martha did not ask you to do anything. Your role as an investor in stocks is to provide the capital (the money) that the business can use for its operations or business expansion.

You can invest in publicly traded companies. Publicly traded means you can buy and sell stocks of companies that are listed (included) in the stock exchange.

Just like with Martha's Pizza Parlor, when you buy the stock you are essentially providing capital for the company to use. And if the company does well, the company may distribute dividends (a portion of the profits of the company) to people who hold their stock.

Another way to earn in stocks is through price appreciation. For example, suppose you originally bought stocks for $40 a share of a company that sells smartphones, then that company experienced a huge demand for their smartphones, because of that it is now a more valuable company and let's say the stock price rose to $48 a share. That is a 20% increase. Should you decide to sell your stock at $48 a share, you would make a 20% return on your money. Remember, you did not lift a finger to earn that 20%. That is the beauty of investing in stocks.

However, suppose that the smartphone was not a hit (maybe because the competitor's phones where much better), the stock price could fall as well.

"You see, even if you don't have a big amount to put up a business and you don't have the time to run a business because you are working, you can still co-own a business by buying its stock. By buying stocks, you get to participate in the potential of the business," William explained.

"I have never thought of it that way. All along I was thinking that I needed to work hard for many years to come up with a big enough capital to put up my own business."

"Thank you for the wonderful dinner. Let's meet Saturday morning for a hike in the mountains. I'll text you the details," William said as he brings out his ringing smartphone and walks towards the door.

Stocks or bonds, they have their upside and their downside. They have different characteristics as you will learn in this book.

Uncertain vs. Less Uncertain Investments

At the hiking trail

"Glad you can make it."

"I have to say, I am a fairly active person but jogging around the park is more of my thing. I am a bit scared that I might fall off a ravine, roll off a steep slope or something. But I am open to this as well," you said to William.

"That is exactly why I brought you here. When you jog around the park, you know you won't fall off a cliff. There is a smaller chance that you will get injured. When hiking, you just don't know. But is sure is more thrilling," William replied.

When you invest in corporate bonds you know from the start how much return you will get and when. Below is a sample of a corporate bond certificate for a fictional company called The Restaurant Company.

BOND CERTIFICATE
THE RESTAURANT COMPANY

$1000   **2.0%** COUPON RATE

The Bearer of this Bond is entitled to receive 20 dollars every 15th of December, every year, from 2016 to 2025 and will receive the face value on 15th December 2025.

When you purchase this $1000-bond you know you are going to receive $20 every 15th of December, yearly, from 2016 to 2025, and the face value of $1000 on 15th of December, 2025. In a bond you know exactly what you are getting and when you will receive it, unlike when buying stocks, where the return varies or is not guaranteed. However the returns can potentially be much bigger than corporate bond returns. You are essentially trading more risk for a possibility of greater returns.

There are still risks, however, when investing in corporate bonds. The risk an investor carries when he/she invests in corporate bonds is the possibility that the company can run into financial trouble and won't have enough funds to pay the coupon or the principal, or the company can even go bankrupt. In which case, the corporate bond investor may recover some or all of her money. The corporate bondholders will get paid before the stockholders/shareholders/stock investors (the owners of the company). Corporate bondholders have priority when it comes to payments over the stockholders. That is why corporate bonds are less risky than stocks. And that is also part of the reason why in general the return you will get from corporate bonds are lower compared to the return you will get from stocks.

"In investing there is a mantra:

In investing, the more risk the investor assumes, the higher the return and vice versa. The higher return is compensation for assuming the added risk," William uttered.

To avoid corporations that are at risk of not being able to make timely payments, look for AAA (Triple-A) rated companies. These are companies that have the least risk of default (not being able to make timely payments), in other words, those with extreme capacity to make timely payments.

Credit rating agencies (agencies that assess the creditworthiness of issuers) assign ratings on the bond or the bond issuer. The table below shows the ratings used by rating agencies.

Agency 1	Agency 2	Agency 3	Credit worthiness
Aaa	AAA	AAA	An obligor has EXTREMELY STRONG capacity to meet its financial commitments.
Aa1	AA+	AA+	An obligor has VERY STRONG capacity to meet its financial commitments. It differs from the highest-rated obligors only to a small degree.
Aa2	AA	AA	
Aa3	AA−	AA−	
A1	A+	A+	An obligor has STRONG capacity to meet its financial commitments but is somewhat more susceptible to the adverse effects of changes in circumstances and economic conditions than obligors in higher-rated categories.
A2	A	A	
A3	A−	A−	
Baa1	BBB+	BBB+	An obligor has ADEQUATE capacity to meet its financial commitments. However, adverse economic conditions or changing circumstances are more likely to lead to a weakened capacity of the obligor to meet its financial commitments.
Baa2	BBB	BBB	
Baa3	BBB−	BBB−	
Ba1	BB+	BB+	An obligor is LESS VULNERABLE in the near term than other lower-rated obligors. However, it faces major ongoing uncertainties and exposure to adverse business, financial, or economic conditions which could lead to the obligor's inadequate capacity to meet its financial commitments.
Ba2	BB	BB	
Ba3	BB−	BB−	
B1	B+	B+	An obligor is MORE VULNERABLE than the obligors rated 'BB', but the obligor currently has

B2	B	B	the capacity to meet its financial commitments. Adverse business, financial, or economic conditions will likely impair the obligor's capacity or willingness to meet its financial commitments.
B3	B-	B-	
Caa	CCC	CCC	An obligor is CURRENTLY VULNERABLE, and is dependent upon favourable business, financial, and economic conditions to meet its financial commitments.
Ca	CC	CC	An obligor is CURRENTLY HIGHLY-VULNERABLE.
	C	C	The obligor is CURRENTLY HIGHLY-VULNERABLE to nonpayment. May be used where a bankruptcy petition has been filed.
C	D	D	An obligor has failed to pay one or more of its financial obligations (rated or unrated) when it became due.

As you can see, companies that are Triple-A rated have extreme capacity to pay (see encircled portion of the table above) and companies rated as "C" (by Agency 1) and "D" (by Agency 2 and Agency 3) are companies that have, in the past, failed to pay at least one of its financial obligations (see underlined portion).

Companies near the top are less risky (less likely to default on their financial obligations) and those near the bottom are riskier (more likely to default on their financial obligations), and based on the investing mantra, that means companies with ratings near the top pay lower returns. Those with ratings near the bottom pay higher returns. The higher return is compensation to the bondholder (those who purchased their bonds) for the added risk that they assume.

In the investment industry there is what is called high-yield bonds. These are what you will see near the bottom of the list. High-yield bonds also go by the name of "junk bonds". They are high yielding because they pay a higher return because they are perceived to be more risky. They are called junk bonds because they are at the bottom of the list, to put it nicely.

We all want the highest returns but there is just a limit to the level of risk your stomach can take. You will experience this when you start investing. Sure, you invested in a bond that pays a higher return than others and you are happy with that. But remember that the higher return is compensation for investing in a company that has a higher chance of not making timely payments or not making any payments at all. Some don't mind that. But others can't sleep well at night because that thought is at the back of their head. In investing, we look at what return to risk combination we are comfortable with (this will become clearer in a later section).

Upon reaching the summit

"The view here is just fantastic, William," you said as you raised both your arms to reach for the sky while turning around as you take a deep breath to soak up the fresh cool air.

"I know and nothing beats the adrenaline rush I get from hiking. The risk was all worth it. Now it's time to climb down," William said with a refreshed face as he points you to the trail down.

With adrenaline still rushing in your vein, you tripped over a stone and nearly rolled down the slope. William helps you up. You only suffered a small cut on your left hand as you used it to prevent your fall. It was not serious. In fact the two of you laughed at the incident because of the thrill it gave both of you.

At the foot of the mountain

"We'll take it easy next time. See me Tuesday afternoon, when you are out from work. Let's just sit on a bench at the park this time," William said as he waved and walk towards his SUV.

As Safe as it Gets Type of Investment

On a bench at the park

"How's your cut?"

"It's nothing. A small price to pay for reaching the summit. I would do it again for the thrill," you replied.

"Tell me, William, is there any way to avoid risk but still get a good return for my money?"

"The closest investments I know that fits your description are government bonds," William replied.

A government bond is the same as a corporate bond. The difference is that government bonds are issued by the US government. And we know the government can always print money to pay you back. That is what makes it very low risk. However, governments are also rated by rating agencies. That means that countries have varying creditworthiness as well. The US has mostly Triple-A ratings (the highest). There are countries that are investment grade and there are those with "junk status", which essentially means there is some doubt as to whether they can repay their debt on time. There have been cases where a sovereign country has defaulted (failed to pay) on its financial obligations.

Government bonds are also called Treasury Securities. There are 3 types.

1. T-Bills or Treasury Bills have short term maturities at 4, 13, 26 and 52 weeks. In other words, they mature in less than a year. T-Bills are a bit different than the bonds I have talked about, in that they are issued at a discount. For example, you can buy a 13-week T-Bill for $995, then after 13 weeks they will pay you $1,000 (a $5 interest). Another way of explaining it is that the T-Bill has a face value of $1,000, but since the maturity is too short to pay coupons, they will just sell it to you for, let's say, $995 (at a discount). Then you will get the face value ($1000) at maturity, in this case after 13 weeks. T-Bills are sometimes called ultrashort bonds. And yes, they can be classified as bonds, but a special case since, they are issued at a discount.

2. T-Notes or Treasury Notes have maturities at 2, 3, 5, 7 and 10 years. They have a $1000 face value and they pay semi-

annual interest. A semi-annual payment means if the coupon is 10% in a $1000 bond then the coupon for the year is $100. Two $50-coupon will be paid with a 6-month interval.

3. T-Bonds or Treasury Bonds are the same as T-Notes but they mature at 30 years. They have a $1000 face value and they pay semi-annual interest.

T-Bill, T-Notes, T-Bonds are essentially all bonds. They mainly differ in maturities (the length of time before the face value is paid out).

The T-Bonds generally pay the highest return among the three but you have to leave your money for 30 years. However, once you bought them you can sell them in a secondary market, if you want, at any time, but the price you will get is not guaranteed.

T-Bills are good for a starting investor to get his/her feet wet in investing because you can get your money back in 1, 3, and 6 months. However, the return is lower compared to the T-Bonds. It may not even be enough to outpace inflation (I will explain inflation later).

Corporate bonds also have varying maturities. But they usually last years (5, 10, 15, 20 years).

In general, the longer the maturity, the higher is the coupon because there is more risk of not getting your money because there is more uncertainty about the financial fitness of the company many years into the future.

"From what you have said so far, it looks to me that there is a spectrum of investments from the safe that pays the low returns to the riskiest but pays high returns," you said to William.

"That is correct," William replied.

"I'll see you tomorrow night, let's eat some hamburgers then," William said as he stood up from the bench and waved goodbye.

The Thief

At the hamburger chain:

"For someone who leads a healthy lifestyle, you're the one who likes hamburgers," you said to William with a hint of sarcasm.

Knowing that you were just trying to be funny, William replied with a smile and a giggle.

"I brought you here to enjoy these juicy hamburgers with melted cheese dripping on the side and with onions that stimulate your taste buds and to point to you a thief," William said with voice that seemed to fade as he mentions "thief".

Your mood changes from jolly to a more serious state of mind. You suddenly became more aware of your surroundings as you scan the people around you with suspicious eyes, and with the voice of William fading.

William snaps his fingers in front of your face. "Are you ok?" he asked.

He continued and said that this thief is so skilled that no money is safe, even if you hide it inside bank vaults.

"The thief is here. The thief is inflation," William whispers.

Inflation simply means if you can buy a hamburger for $5 today, that exact same hamburger will cost more than $5, let's say, 5 years from today. That means the value of your money has decreased, because if it did not, then you can still purchase the exact same hamburger for $5 5 years from today. But because it did then your $5 is simply not enough.

Look at it this way:

If there is no inflation, the value of your money (represented by the water inside the container) will be the same 5 years into the future (see illustration on the next page).

If there is NO Inflation

Value of your money today

Value of your money after 5 years

When there is inflation, it is like "Mr. Inflation" used a drill to bore a hole near the bottom of the container. The value of your money will be less in the future (see next page).

With Inflation

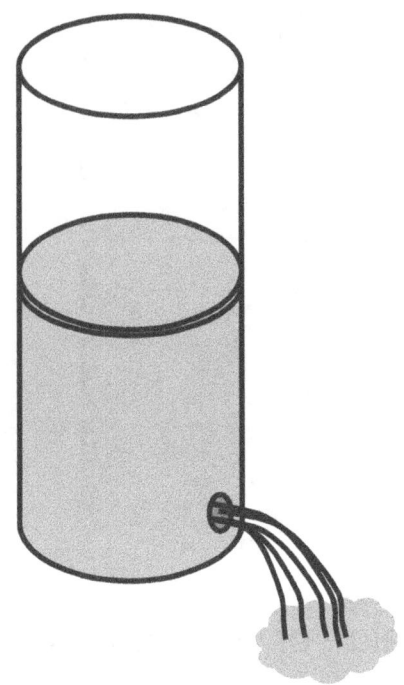

Value of your
money today

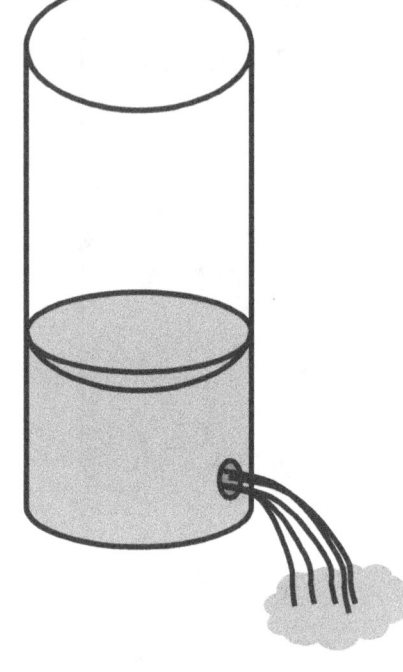

Value of your money
after 5 years

That means your $2,000 today that doesn't grow will only be worth $1,808 after 5 years (assuming inflation of 2%). Do not worry about the calculation. What is important for you to know now is that you are getting poorer due to inflation.

If however you are investing your money, you can maintain your buying power. In the illustration below, the investment return is represented by the water flowing from the faucet into the container.

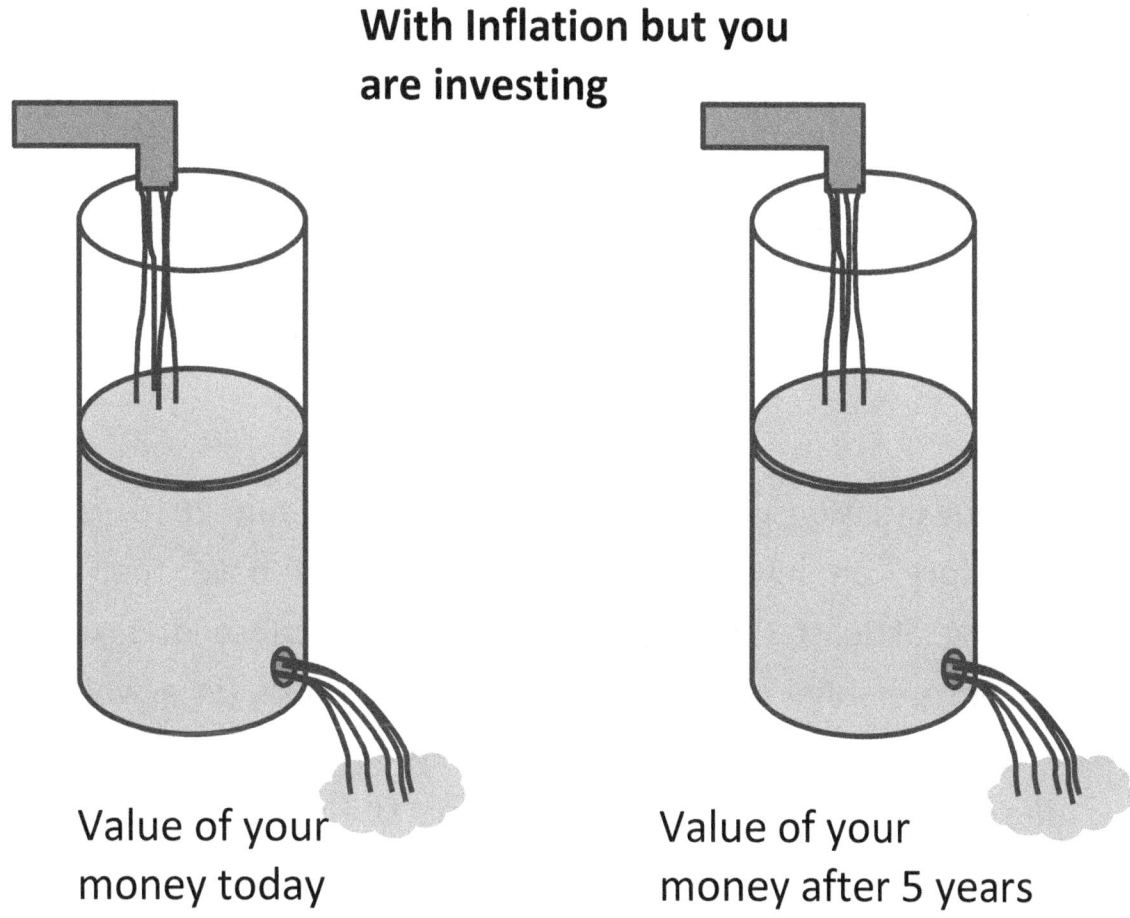

With Inflation but you are investing

Value of your money today

Value of your money after 5 years

In other words, the return from your investments will help you to maintain or even increase your purchasing power. If inflation is at 2%, your investment should be earning at least 2% to keep pace with inflation, and more than 2% to be able to grow your purchasing power.

Those who do not invest will unknowingly have their cash value eaten away by inflation. And that is a tragedy.

This is a problem for everyone, both the not so rich and maybe much more for the rich because they have more cash. Imagine a relatively not so rich person who has $100,000 cash. That person will lose $2,000 in value if the inflation is 2%. A rich person with $10,000,000 cash will lose $200,000 in value. It is like they are losing money without spending a single penny.

Current inflation in the United States (as of July 2016) is 0.84%. Therefore, an investor at this time should have their money earning at least 0.84% (and even more because of taxes). The current personal savings account rate is 0.03% (in a well-known bank). That's not enough. The investor's cash will lose its value due to inflation. Not only that, the US inflation average from 2000 to 2012 is at 2.5%.

"That's why money is not safe in banks," you whispered.

Let's see if bonds and stocks can outpace the US inflation average of 2.5% (see table below).

Asset Class	Average Yearly Return
Government Bonds	3.12%
Corporate Bonds	3.67%
Stocks	9.03%

Data used: 2006-2015 average

It looks like all of them can outpace inflation.

But which asset class would you choose?

If you say stocks, I don't blame you. A 9.03% return is far better than 3.67% or 3.12%.

But why the difference in returns? It is because they carry different risks (see table below).

Asset Class	Riskiness	Riskiness Explained
Government Bonds	Least risky of the 3	The US government or any government can always print money to pay you back
Corporate Bonds	less risky than stocks, more risky than gov't bonds	If the company goes bankrupt, the bondholders (those who own the bonds) get paid first over the stockholders (those who own shares/stocks of the company). The bondholders have a higher chance to recover some, if not all their money
Stocks	most risky of the 3	The stockholders are paid last (if

		there is money left after paying the bondholders) Shareholders have the highest risk of losing their money

From the table above, the least risky is government bonds, the most risky is stocks, and corporate bonds rank in the middle.

Remember our mantra in investing (repeated below)

In investing, the more risk the investor assumes, the higher the return and vice versa. The higher return is compensation for assuming the added risk.

That means in terms of returns, stocks would pay the most, government bonds the least, and corporate bonds in between (see table below).

Asset Class	Riskiness	Average Yearly Return
Stocks	Most risky	9.03%
Corporate Bonds	In-between	3.67%
Government Bonds	Least risky	3.12%

A note on bonds:

As long as you hold bonds to maturity (if you have a bond that has a 2 year term, you hold it for 2 years) and given that the issuer of the bond does not default, it's hard to imagine how you would lose money.

Selling your bond before maturity is a different case. Yes. You can sell your 2-year bond at any time. To explain a bit: In general, if you own a bond and interest rates go up (the Federal Reserve controls this) and you sold, you may lose money. On the other hand, if interests rates go down, it is probable that you can make more money that what you would get if you held the bond to maturity. But don't worry about this for now. Again, what you need to know now is: barring default and if you held the bond to maturity, you won't lose money by investing in bonds.

"The last place millionaires would put their money is in cash deposited in banks," you're the one who mentioned it this time.

"The interest paid by the banks on our money may not outpace inflation and so, we become poorer or less rich without spending a single penny," you continued.

"You are learning well," William replied feeling satisfied.

"William, I have gotten very interested with stocks"

"I knew you would. Let's talk more about that this weekend. I will send you a text message on where to meet and what time," William said as he stood up and walks away.

An Emotional Investment

At the movie theater

"A horror movie?! Are trying to give me a heart attack, William?"

"Don't be a chicken, come on," William replied with a smirk.

While watching the film your popcorn was almost halved because you jerked from being startled and scared. You also almost went out of the theater, if only you were watching alone. But you have to put on a brave face for William. It is simply embarrassing to walk out.

The highest returns are achievable in stocks. However, investing in stocks is *very* emotional. The table below is about an investor who puts in $1,000 by end of 2005 in the stock market. He is very excited to invest in the stock market for the very first time and he can already see his money growing in his mind. Follow the emotions of the investor and his possible action as the years pass by (see table on the next page).

Year	Stock Market Return (S&P 500)	Value of $1,000 investment	Emotions	Possible action by investor
2005		$1,000	optimistic and happy to be investing for the first time	Invested $1,000 by end of 2005
2006	15.61%	$1,156	happy because his money grew	none
2007	5.48%	$1,220	happier because his money grew even more	none
2008	-36.55%	$774	fearful, because from $1,220 his money went down to $774 (an almost $500 loss)	Sell at a loss because of fear and pain of having his initial investment lose 23% (from $1,000 down to $774
2009	25.94%	$974	fear turned into optimism	none, had he not sold in 2008
2010	14.82%	$1,119	happy because money grew	none, had he not sold in 2008
2011	2.10%	$1,142	happy because money grew	none, had he not sold in 2008
2012	15.89%	$1,324	happy because money grew	none, had he not sold in 2008
2013	32.15%	$1,749	happy because money grew	none, had he not sold in 2008
2014	13.52%	$1,986	happy because money grew	none, had he not sold in 2008
2015	1.36%	$2,013	happy to have **doubled** his money	sold stock after **doubling money**

*Returns presented are actual returns of the S&P 500.

As you can see, if the stock investor held on to his stock up to 2015, he would double his money. However, the investor must have the courage to *not* give in to the pain and fear of losing money in 2008 (the truth is he has not lost money, it's only paper losses if he does not sell, but to him it very much feels like he is losing money). If the investor sold in 2008, he would realize a loss of 23% on his initial investment instead of doubling it had he held until end of 2015.

The stock market is an emotional investment.

"I see where you are going with this. This movie is another one of your lessons. You brought me here to show me that emotions like fear can affect us and our actions, just like when I spilled the popcorn on the person sitting beside me when I got startled and scared, and when I almost walked out because of fear," you told William.

"Very perceptive," William approved.

"Emotions can cloud our judgement," he continued.

However, the stock market is the rockstar of investments. That is why there are many television shows talking about stocks. Why is it the rockstar of investments? You only need to look at the chart below, to know why.

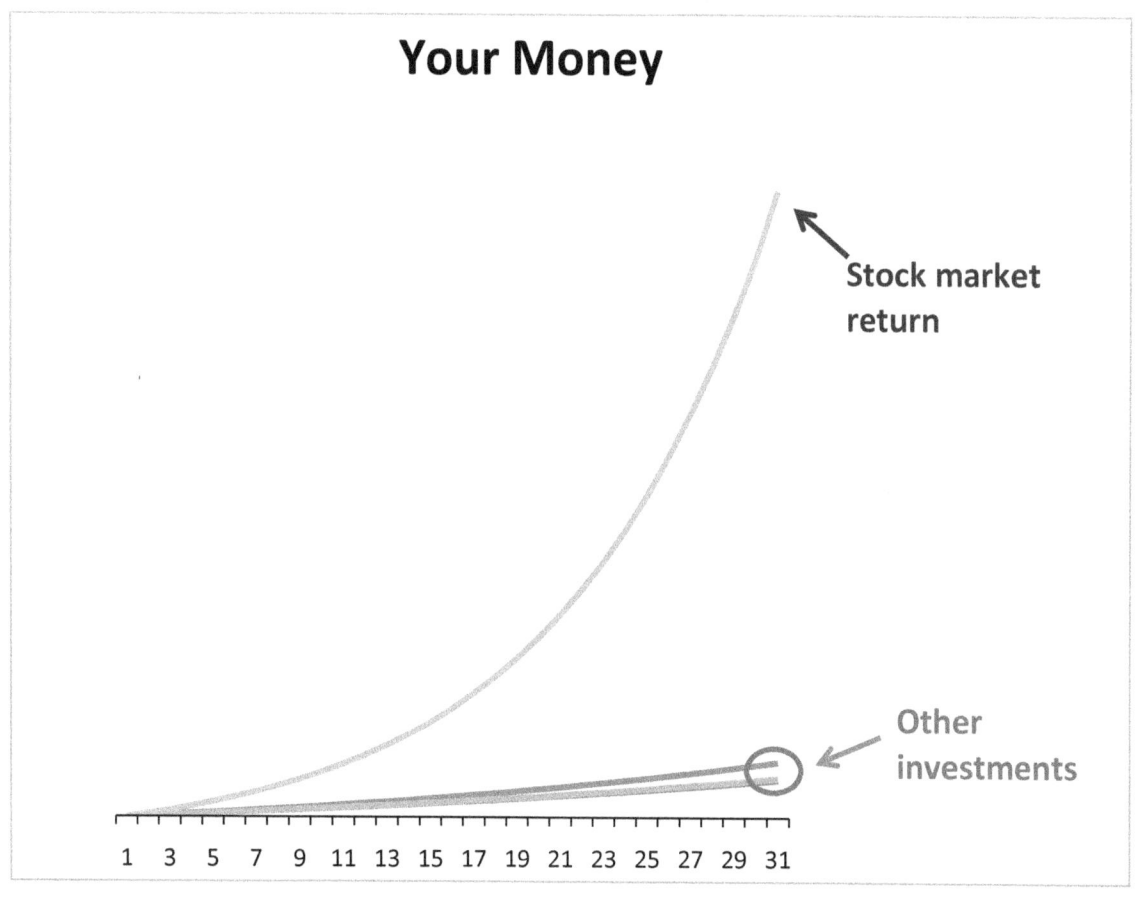

*Other investments here include government bonds, corporate bonds, and Certificates of Deposit

That kind of spectacular return is deserving of our attention. Bonds and CDs simply don't compare. The stock market is one's best bet to accumulating wealth. *More to discover ahead.*

"Let us have coffee again tomorrow," William said.

I Have the Money, Where Should I Put It

At the coffee shop

"I have been a saver since and I have stashed some extra cash, William. What investment vehicle should I choose?" you asked even before taking your first sip of your coffee.

"That is a good question," William replied.

For a beginning investor you should focus on just the major asset classes—stocks and bonds (bonds here include T-Bills). Again, you can always explore other asset classes later.

Here is a simplified guide on where to invest your money (see next page):

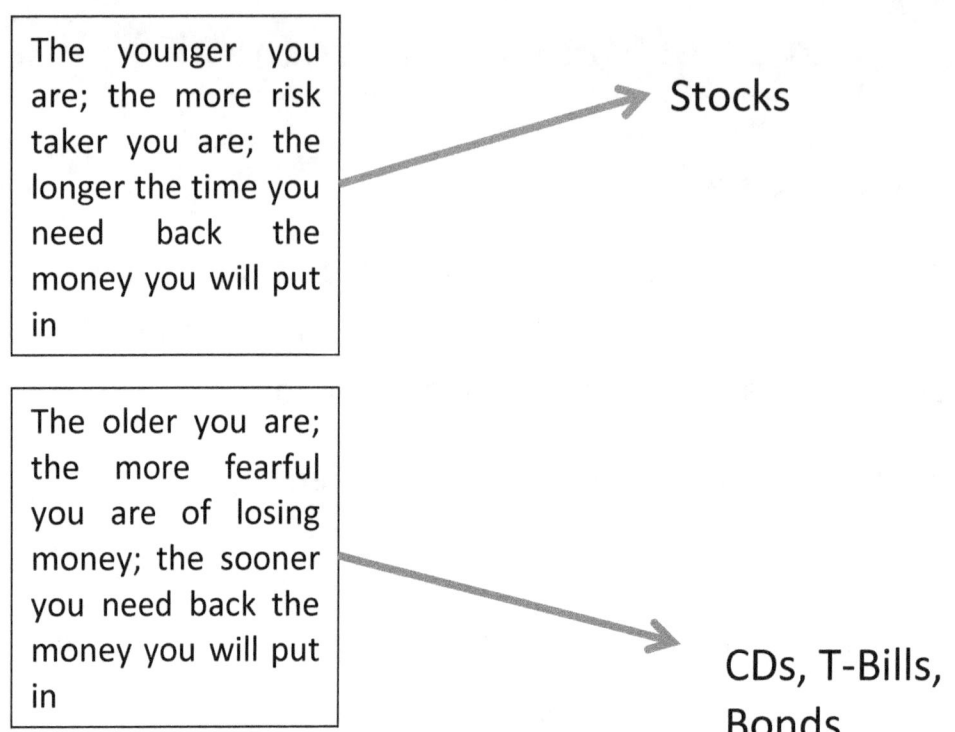

Thus, allocate more to stocks if you are young, a risk taker, and when you won't need the money for a long time. Otherwise, allocate more towards T-Bills and Bonds.

You can be described as an aggressive type or a risk averse type (dislikes risk) of an investor. The table below shows the general attributes of each and a short explanation.

Investor type	Attributes	Remarks
Aggressive	young	has more time before retirement, has more time to recover if he/she makes an investment mistake
	risk taker	Willing to take more risk for higher returns
	Can keep money invested for an extended period	The longer the time money is in the stock market the higher the chance that it will appreciate in value
Risk Averse	Old (not so young)	The closer an investor is to retirement, the less risk he/she should take

Has less time to recover from an |

		investment mistake. Which means if the investor loses money he/she will be affected negatively because his/her high earning years are already behind him/her, it will be difficult to make up for the loss. Also, he/she is nearing the stage where he/she won't have active income anymore
	scared of losing money	Investing in stocks can be emotional for many, if the investor gets scared he/she will sell at a loss
	Needs money back soon	T-Bills, CDs, and 1-2 yr. T-Notes are short term investments, the investor can get his/her money back early

Nothing is set in stone. For an example on the extreme side, a person at age 60 should be risk averse (according to the table above), but if that person is *willing* (wants to) and can take on more risk (i.e. *has capacity*, meaning: has a lot of extra cash, so no problem even if the he loses money), then he can be considered as an aggressive investor. Note the emphasis on willing and having capacity.

In investing, you should know your risk appetite.

How do you know your risk appetite (i.e. are you a risk taker or risk averse)? Look at the illustration on the next page and answer this question: Suppose you have a $5,000 investment, and given the highest possible gain and the biggest possible loss (shown on the chart on the next page) on your investment, which of the following scenarios are you most comfortable with? Is it with A, B or C?

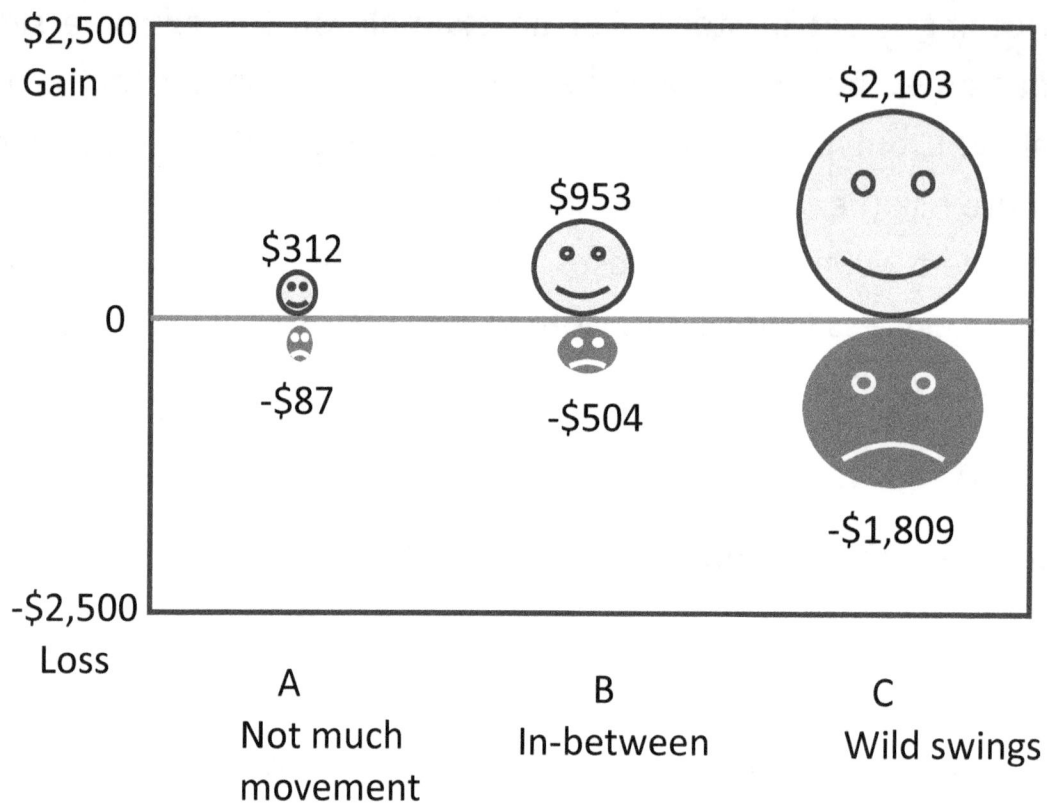

Here is the meaning of your answer:

What is your risk appetite?	
If you answered C	You are a risk taker
If you answered A	You are risk averse (dislikes risk)
If you answered B	You are in-between

An investor will need this when he/she starts to allocate his/her money in to the different asset classes later on.

Aside from your risk appetite, your financial goal should also influence where you should put your money and how much of it. The table below shows some of financial goals an investor may have along with possible investment vehicles that can meet his/her financial goal, and a short explanation.

Financial Goal	Possible Investment Vehicle	Remarks
A 25 year old wanting to save for retirement (long term)	Stocks, high-yield bonds, long-term bonds (10 to 30 year maturities)	Long term bonds usually have higher interest rates than short-term bonds Stocks provide the biggest returns in the long run High-yield bonds provide higher returns that low

		risk bonds
Put my child's college funds away for 5 years in a financial instrument that is very safe, liquid and earns interest higher than inflation	5-year US government bonds	US Government Bonds are considered risk-free or at least very low risk and it can earn interest above inflation
Earn higher interest than a personal savings account on a $15,000 down payment money for a car to be bought 4 months from now	T-Bills	Ideal for short-term (less than a year) investment, very low risk, very liquid and can earn interest higher than a deposit account

For people asking what liquid means, it means you can easily pull out your investment and convert it to cash.

There is an investment vehicle for every reasonable financial goal. The table below shows a general guide.

If the Financial Goal:	Suited Asset Class
Is long-term	Stocks and long-term bonds
Is short-term	T-Bills, short-term bonds
Demands big growth	Stocks or high-yield bonds
Requires capital preservation	Bonds (high quality/high rated bonds, i.e. those that have low risk of default)

"I think I got this. Where I should put my money depends on my risk appetite, my financial goal and my age," you said to William.

"That is correct," William approved.

"Let's meet tomorrow. I will text you the details where," William said.

A Tailor Fit Investment Portfolio

At the tailor shop

"I have been a loyal customer of this shop since I was 27," William said.

"So, this is where you get your nice suit," you replied impressed.

"I only look good in a suit because it fits me, otherwise, I would look awkward or lousy," William said in a confident voice.

"I did not say you look good in your suit. I just said nice suit. Just kidding. But why did you bring me here?"

"You asked where you should put your money. The answer to that is in a collection of assets that *fits* you."

The table below shows sample asset allocations (how you divide your investible money into different asset classes) with 2 combinations for each type of risk.

Note: When we say bonds from here on, we generally refer to high quality/high rated bonds, unless stated otherwise.

How to use the Asset Allocation table:

If you are a risk taker	Refer to Aggressive Risk column
If you are risk averse (dislikes risk)	Refer to Low Risk column
If you are in-between	Refer to Moderate Risk column

Sample Asset Allocation

	Low Risk		Moderate Risk		Aggressive Risk	
Treasury Bills	30%	30%	20%	10%	0%	10%
Bonds	40%	30%	30%	40%	30%	20%
US Stocks	30%	30%	40%	40%	60%	70%
International Stocks	0%	10%	10%	10%	10%	0%

(**NOTE:** These are for educational purposes only)

International stocks are stocks outside of the United States. Adding international stocks (considered as more risky than US stocks) can boost growth and provide added diversification (I will explain diversification later).

In the Sample Asset Allocation table above, the "Low Risk" allocation is generally recommended for people nearing retirement, "Moderate Risk" allocation for middle-aged persons, and "Aggressive Risk" allocation for younger persons.

As you can see, when you make allocations you will have a combination of asset classes (stocks is one asset class, bonds is another asset class) and this combination or collection of asset classes is called a portfolio. The reason for mixing asset classes is to make the portfolio fit the needs (risk appetite, age and financial goal) of the investor and also to provide diversification.

Diversification

Diversification is the idea of not putting all your eggs in one basket. Diversification protects you from catastrophic losses. For example: Suppose you put all your investible money into one stock. Then that company goes bankrupt. In that case, you will suffer severe losses. You may lose all your money or may only recover a portion. Diversification (spreading your money into different asset classes) can protect you from such severe losses. In a diversified portfolio, even if one asset class declines in value, the other asset class(es) may appreciate in value to offset that decline (see table below).

	Invested Dollar Amount	% Gain or Loss	$ Gain or Loss
Treasury Bills	$2,000	+0.21%	+$4.20
Bonds	$3,000	-2.24%	-$67.20
US Stocks	$4,000	+5.3%	+$212.00
Int'l Stocks	$1,000	-0.12%	-$1.20
		Total Gain or Loss =	+$147.8

From the table above, you can see the benefits of a diversified portfolio as it helps to limit your losses. The $67.20 loss from Bonds and $1.20 loss from International Stocks are offset by the gains from US Stocks ($212.00) and T-Bills ($4.20). The resulting performance of the portfolio is an overall gain of $147.8.

Going back to the assets allocation table (presented again below):

Sample Asset Allocation

	Low Risk		Moderate Risk		Aggressive Risk	
Treasury Bills	30%	30%	20%	10%	0%	10%
Bonds	40%	30%	30%	40%	30%	20%
US Stocks	30%	30%	40%	40%	60%	70%
International Stocks	0%	10%	10%	10%	10%	0%

Notice from the sample asset allocation that the more aggressive the portfolio, the more is allocated to stocks. And for a lower risk portfolio, less money is allocated to stocks and more is allocated to the less risky assets (Bonds and T-Bills).

Moreover, the if you need your money back sooner, maybe because you are nearing retirement, you allocate your money more on Treasury Bills and short-term Bonds (1-2 year maturities), which are short-term, relatively lower risk, and liquid investments (just like in the Low Risk allocation above where 60% to 70% are allocated to a combination of T-Bills and Bonds).

You can tweak the allocations. For example, if you are a middle-aged person, the original sample asset allocation recommends the Moderate Risk Portfolio for you (see table below).

	Moderate Risk	
Treasury Bills	20%	10%
Bonds	30%	40%
US Stocks	40%	40%
International Stocks	10%	10%

However, despite the recommended allocation, if you want higher returns and you are willing to and can take on more risk (i.e. you are a risk taker with financial capacity), you can decrease your allocation on bonds by 10% (underlined), for example, and transfer that 10% to stocks (encircled). See table below.

	Original		Tweaked	
	Moderate Risk		Moderate Risk	
Treasury Bills	20%	10%	20%	10%
Bonds	30%	40%	20%	30%
US Stocks	40%	40%	50%	40%
International Stocks	10%	10%	10%	20%

The Tweaked asset allocation essentially increases your exposure to a historically better yielding asset, which is stocks, but it will also expose you more to the volatility in returns (possible wild swings in gains or losses) associated stocks.

"I think you are ready to create your own investment portfolio," said William.

"A portfolio that fits me. I guess so," you replied.

You can now *go into action.*

There are many types of investors. Some want complete control of their investments, some want to take it easy and just put money into a fund and have the fund manager do the investing for them. Whatever type of investor you are, the following sections will help you *get started on investing.*

Captain of the Ship Investor

For those who want to be the 'Captain' of their investments (those who want complete control over his/her investments), here's how you can get started.

1. Open an online discount brokerage account (you will need this to buy stocks and bonds).
2. Fund your account.
3. Know your risk appetite and financial goal.
4. Determine the asset allocation that meets your risk appetite and financial goal.
5. Start building your portfolio by buying individual bonds and stocks based on your asset allocation. This may require some skill (i.e. stock picking and picking of individual bonds)
6. Invest more money as you please. Rebalance your portfolio from time to time.

That's it!

One good thing about making your own decisions is that you avoid fund management fees and other charges that eat into your overall return. But, you need to work on your investing skills.

Here is a generalized example:

Investor Profile (fictional)

Name: Jim

Gender: Male

Age: 35 years old

Job: Employee at marketing company

Risk appetite: In-between

Financial Goal: to save for a retirement fund (retire at age 65) (long term)

Preferred Level of engagement in managing own portfolio: hands-on

Starting investment amount: $10,000

Based on the investor profile, a possible asset allocation is presented below:

	Moderate Risk		
	% Allocation	Dollar Allocation	Remarks
Treasury Bills	20%	$2,000	Will allow the investor to have ready access to a very liquid assets with very low risk, in case he needs it for an emergency
Bonds	40%	$4,000	Will provide the investor with decent return that is above inflation while keeping the money on a moderate risk investment vehicle
US Stocks	35%	$3,500	Will provide the investor growth by having exposure to stocks
International Stocks	5%	$500	Will provide the investor exposure to more growth outside the US; will also provide investor added diversification for his portfolio
	Total = $10,000		

Additional Remarks: At age 35, Jim's portfolio essentially has 60% in bonds (Treasury Bills are considered very short-term bonds) and 40% in stocks. This allocation will satisfy the investors in-between risk appetite and his long term financial goal of having a retirement fund.

The investor in this case will just keep on adding money to his portfolio, keeping in mind to maintain the asset allocation, as long as his financial goal or risk appetite remain the same.

Fast forward 3 years: The investor's stock return is more significant compared to the other asset classes. Today, his portfolio looks like this (See table below).

	Moderate Risk				
	A	B	C	D	D-A
	Original % Allocation	Dollar Amount Today	% Allocation Today due to the performance of the portfolio	Rebalanced Dollar allocation (Total x Column A)	
Treasury Bills	20%	$2,100	17.8%	$2,360	increase by $260
Bonds	40%	$4,500	38.14%	$4,720	increase by $220
US Stocks	35%	$4,500	38.14%	$4,130	reduce by $370
Int'l Stocks	5%	$700	5.92%	$590	reduce by $110
	Total= $11,800				

If you compare Column A with Column C, the proportion is now different from the original. The proportion of stocks (both US and Int'l) increased from 40% (35% US + 5% Int'l) to 44.06% (38.14% US + 5.92% Int'l) and the proportion of Bonds (both Treasury Bills, which is considered as very short-term bonds, and long-term

Bonds) decreased from 60% (40% Bonds + 20% T-Bills) to 55.94% (38.14% Bonds + 17.8% T-Bills).

The change in proportion, in this case, where stocks increased in weight will make the portfolio of the investor more risky. This increased risk may not meet his in-between risk appetite. With increased weight on stocks, he may experience price swings that he may not be comfortable with, and may cause him to make emotional and irrational decisions that may have negative financial impact. Moreover, the increased weight in stocks and consequently the decreased weight in bonds, in general, may not sit well with his age at 35 where he should be more moderate in taking risks. There is a reason why we identify our risk appetite in the first place.

It is therefore recommended that the investor rebalances his portfolio in order to revert to the original asset allocation that meets his risk appetite and financial goal.

To rebalance a portfolio, the investor will do buying and selling of portions of his portfolio. The last column of the table above shows the changes he should make. For example, since US stocks has a bigger weight now, he should sell some of his stocks to produce an amount close to $370 dollars (see last column of the table above). He should also reduce his International Stocks by selling portions of it to come up with an amount somewhere near $110. Then he should use the $480 ($370 + $110) proceed to purchase $260 worth of T-Bills and $220 worth of Bonds. These actions will make his portfolio in line again with the original asset allocation that meets his risk appetite and financial goal. Rebalancing can be done yearly.

If however, the investor has changed his mind and now has a new financial goal or his risk appetite has changed, he would need to create a new portfolio that will suit his new financial situation.

Here is another example, this time for a younger investor:

Investor Profile (fictional)

Name: Diane

Gender: Female

Age: 23 years old

Job: accountant

Risk appetite: Aggressive

Financial Goal: come up with $46,000 to be used as 20% down payment for a house in 10 years' time (medium term)

Preferred Level of engagement in managing own portfolio: hands-on

Starting investment amount: $10,000

Based on the investor profile, a possible asset allocation is presented below:

	Aggressive Risk	
	% Allocation	Dollar Allocation
Treasury Bills	0%	$0.0
Bonds	30%	$3,000
US Stocks	60%	$6,000
International Stocks	10%	$1,000
		Total = $10,000

At a young age 23 and with a financial goal that is medium term and demanding in terms of needed growth, her portfolio essentially has 30% in Bonds and 70% in Stocks. This aggressive asset allocation (with 70% in Stocks) sits well with her age, risk appetite and financial goal of having big money by the end of ten years.

The investor in this case will just keep on adding money to her portfolio, while keeping in mind to maintain the asset allocation as long as her financial goal and risk appetite remain the same. Rebalancing here follows the same process as with our first investor, Jim.

If however, Diane changed her mind and now has a new financial goal or her risk appetite has changed, she would need to make a new portfolio that will suit her new financial situation.

Awareness and control

These are the two best reasons for having a 'Captain of the ship' investments style. You have awareness on what is happening or what has happened to your portfolio and you have control to make the changes that you want.

Autopilot Investing

For those who want an 'Autopilot' investing style because they want to take it easy, here's what you can do to get started.

1. Open an online discount brokerage account (you will need this to buy mutual funds*).
2. Fund your account.
3. Know your risk appetite and financial goal.
4. Determine the asset allocation that meets your risk appetite** and financial goal.
5. Start buying mutual funds to build a portfolio based on the asset allocation that you have determined.
6. Invest more money as you please. Rebalance your portfolio from time to time.

*What is a mutual fund? It is a pooled fund. Remember you put in money in the mutual fund? There are probably tens of thousands of you who put in money. The money collected from all of you is massive and a fund manager uses that money to buy assets. In a mutual fund, a fund manager takes your place in making decisions on what to buy and sell, when to buy and sell. That is why this is an 'autopilot' investing style. You just put in the money and a fund manager actively manages it for you.

**There are mutual funds that will fit nicely in every investor's portfolio, given his/her risk appetite and financial goal. The table below shows the recommended type of mutual fund depending on your risk appetite.

Risk Appetite	Recommended Type of Mutual Fund	This Fund invests
Risk taker	Stocks Fund (also called Equity Fund)	Purely in stocks (a portfolio of stocks)
Risk averse	Bond Fund	Purely in bonds (a portfolio of bonds)
In-between	Balanced Fund	Usually 60% bonds and 40% stocks
Very risk averse	Money Market Fund (some call it ultrashort bond fund)	Mostly T-Bills, Certificates of Deposit

But since we will create a portfolio that fits the financial situation of an investor, we will have a mix of these mutual funds. You will see that in the example later on.

When choosing a mutual fund, choose the fund that has good historical performance and low expense ratio. The online discount brokerage will have this information. All else equal, funds with the lowest expense ratio will help you keep more of what you earn.

Let us look at a "take it easy" investor:

Investor Profile (fictional)

Name: Joe

Gender: Male

Age: 35 years old

Job: Store manager at local supermarket

Risk appetite: In-between

Financial Goal: to save for a retirement fund (retire at age 65) (long term)

Preferred Level of engagement in managing own portfolio: minimal (too busy at work)

Starting cash investment amount: $10,000

Based on the investor's profile, a possible asset allocation is presented below. Unlike with Jim who individually picks stocks and bonds, here there is a fund manager (an expert) that does the thinking and the work for Joe.

	Moderate Risk	
	% Allocation	Dollar Allocation
Money Market Fund or ultrashort bond fund	20%	$2,000
Bond Fund	40%	$4,000
Domestic Equity Fund (equity means stocks)	35%	$3,500

International Equity Fund	5%	$500
	Total = $10,000	

The downside of investing in mutual funds is the management fee and other charges. But for someone who does not have the time or patience to manage his/her own, this can be the appropriate portfolio.

And since this is a portfolio, you will need to rebalance at least yearly. A once a year rebalancing won't take much of your time. (Rebalancing is explained under the "Captain of the Ship Investor" section, in case you skipped it).

While it is possible to just buy *only a* balanced fund (i.e. a standalone balanced fund) if you really don't have the time or patience, however, creating your own portfolio is like tailor fitting the investment to your personal financial situation. Plus it has the added protection you get from greater diversification. A balanced fund can be bought by persons who have varying financial situations in life (like having different financial goals/needs and risk appetite). A 60% bonds and 40% stocks balanced fund cannot simply very closely fit to the situation of all the buyers of the balanced fund. It cannot meet the nuance of every investor. Thus, creating a portfolio makes sense.

Another 'Autopilot' investing style is investing in a portfolio of exchange traded funds (ETFs). Here is what you need to do to get started:

1. Open an online discount brokerage account (you will need this to buy ETFs*).
2. Fund your account.
3. Know your risk appetite and financial goal.
4. Determine the asset allocation that meets your risk appetite and financial goal.
5. Start buying ETFs to build a portfolio based on your asset allocation.
6. Invest more money as you please. Rebalance your portfolio from time to time.

*ETFs mimic the composition of the index it is tracking. For example, an S&P 500 ETF will buy exactly the composition of the

S&P 500 (all 500 companies). Whatever the performance of the S&P 500 index, the ETF will have similar performance. ETFs are not actively managed, unlike a mutual fund, but they still have management fees.

Let's look at another "take it easy" investor:

Investor Profile (fictional)

Name: Rachel

Gender: Female

Age: 22 years old

Job: proprietor of a startup company that sells clothes, shoes and bags online

Risk appetite: aggressive

Financial Goal: to have big enough money to have a long-term lease on warehouse after 10 years (medium term)

Preferred Level of engagement in managing own portfolio: minimal (too busy chasing dream)

Starting investment amount: $10,000

Based on the investor's profile, a possible asset allocation is presented below.

	Aggressive Risk	
	% Allocation	Dollar Allocation
T-Bills Index	0%	$0.0
Bond Index	30%	$3,000
Domestic Equity Index (equity means stocks)	50%	$5,000
International Equity Index	20%	$2,000
	Total = $10,000	

This allocation sits well with Rachel's aggressive appetite, age, and the big growth demand of her financial goal. Being that this is investing in a portfolio of ETFs gives her the benefit of diversification and releases her from spending too much time thinking about her investments, as she is very busy with her business startup.

ETFs still have some management fees. Consider purchasing ETFs with low expense ratio. All else equal, funds with the lowest expense ratio will help you keep more of what you earn.

Note: You will have a lot of choices within the online broker trading platform. That's good and that could be a problem as well because it's hard to choose with so many. Try not to get overwhelmed. As a beginning investor, keep it simple.

Epilogue

It was a surreal afternoon. You are standing on your lawn as if expecting someone. After a moment, a limousine pulls over. The driver went out and opens the door for the passenger.

An old man steps out (hair all white, wearing a nice suit).

"So this is your house," the old man said in a mild voice as he looks towards the facade of the house. He paused briefly as if trying to assess the house.

"It is elegant."

"Yeah, just like what I saw 3 decades ago…"

Important Reminder to a Beginning Investor

As a beginning investor, start with a small amount to get your feet wet. Spread your purchases. Do not put in all your investible funds in one go. When you get the hang of it and begin to see profits, you can increase your investments. Do not be in a hurry to get rich. It may create the opposite effect. Patience is a must. There is no get rich quick advice here, only get rich prudently.

Investing is a habit.

Investing is not just having the knowledge, equally important, if not more important is having the habits of a successful investor.

Read on. More to discover ahead.

Expanding Your Investment Portfolio

There are many more investment vehicles out there. I will briefly explain some of them below. Note however that you should focus your efforts on the material I have presented prior. That will help you get started on investing and on your way to realizing your true wealth potential. The following investment vehicles however are something to look forward to when you become a more experienced investor.

REIT or Real Estate Investment Trust

Sounds fancy but it's simple. If you don't have a lot of cash to buy a rental property, you can put smaller amounts in REITs. REITs pool money from thousands of investors (just like mutual funds) and the money gathered is massive and the REITs use that money to buy many rental properties, commercial spaces, hotels, to name a few. REITs may even provide mortgages. The income from these properties and other investments is distributed to the owners of the REITs, like you.

If you want to invest in real estate but don't have a lot of cash, REITs may suit your investment need. Plus it is very liquid (i.e.

easily convertible to cash). REITs can be easily bought and sold, just like a stock, unlike if you buy a piece of land or property, you cannot easily find a buyer at your price point.

Real Estate

If you have the cash and you don't need the money anytime soon, you can probably buy real estate. You can rent it out or you can flip it.

Preferred Shares

We have talked about bonds and stocks in this book. Preferred shares are like a hybrid of stocks and bonds. It is like a bond because it pays out dividends (like coupons) but it also represents some sort of ownership of a company.

Art

Often times this is the choice of the rich as art really appreciates in price overtime. But it has storage costs and there are fakes out there.

Commodities

Commodities refer to gold, silver, wheat, oil, etc. People make money trading commodities.

There are a lot more like FOREX, options, swaps and other derivatives.

Investments Reserved for the Rich

Hedge Fund

This is almost like a mutual fund except that to be able to invest in this fund you need to have:

- earned income that exceeded $200,000 (or $300,000 together with a spouse) in each of the prior two years, and reasonably expects the same for the current year,

- OR has a net worth over $1 million, either alone or together with a spouse (excluding the value of the person's primary residence). a net worth of $1,000,000 (which excludes the value of your primary residence)

Those conditions came from the US SEC (US Securities and Exchange Commission). They further explain to the would be accredited investor that:

"These offerings, sometimes referred to as private placements, involve unique risks and you should be aware that you could lose your entire investment"

The US SEC further requires that an accredited investor be *sophisticated* in financial and business matters so that he/she can assess the merits and risks of the prospective investment.

The US SEC, in my opinion, requires the investors in hedge funds to be rich not to keep the not so rich out but to protect the small investors, because hedge funds employ risky strategies like taking on leverage.

Private Equity Fund

Private equity funds look to buy companies (usually distressed, meaning not doing well but has potential) using some money from their rich investors and a bunch of borrowed money from the banks. They streamline the companies and after sometime sell them for a much higher price than they originally bought them. It is like flipping a house.

Venture Capital

Venture capital looks for promising startups and gives them money to make their concepts a reality or expand their operations on the condition that the venture capitalist will own, let's say, 60%

of the company and will have the final say on important decisions of the company. If the startup proves to be a success the venture capitalist will sell the company and split the proceeds with the owner.

This can also be a risky investment since startups have a high probability of failure.

Here is What to Do When You are Not Yet Rich and Financially Sophisticated

Until you are rich enough and sophisticated enough to invest in the investments reserved for the rich, you should start small and learn your way to financial sophistication.

Start your learning to financial sophistication by honing your skill on the stock market.

The stock market is by far the best investment vehicle to accumulate wealth. A $100 left alone in the stock market at the start of the year 1928 will exponentially grow into $294,061 in year 2015. That means the money grew 2,941x.

And, investing in stocks can be learned.

My book can help you get started. It is a beginner's guide to investing in the stock market. If you're new to stocks and you don't know what you to do, my book can teach you how to select stocks like a pro.

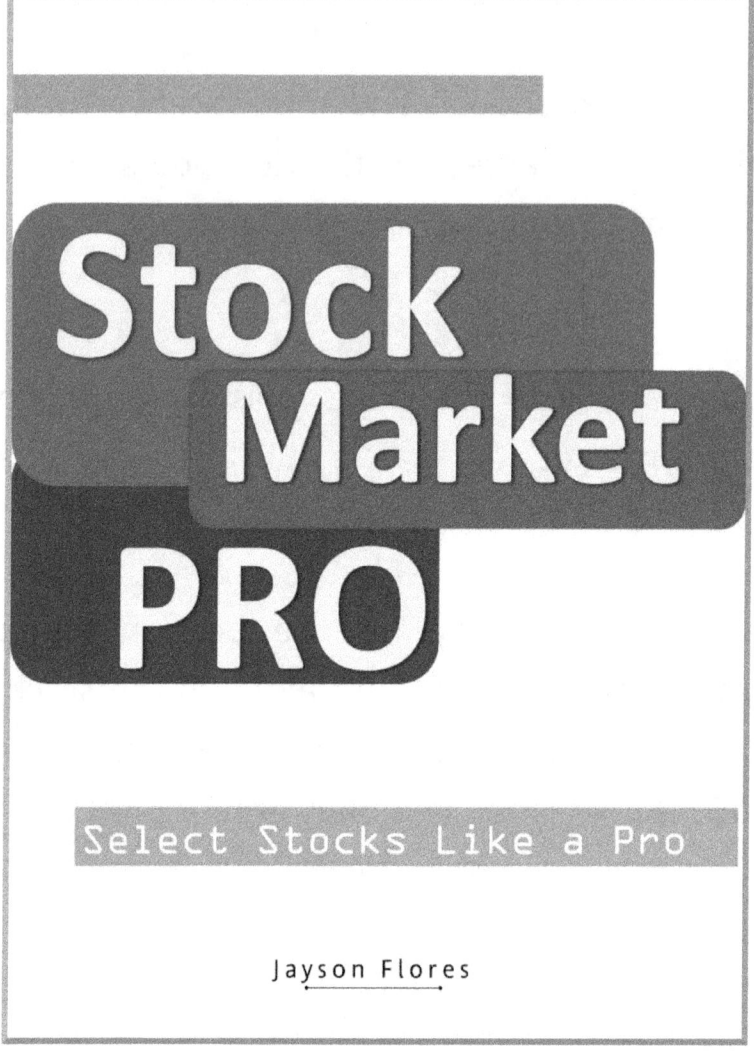

Available online

Not investing is not an option

Everyone has a chance to get rich in this world. That is why a lot of millionaires are self-made.

I wish you luck in your investments!

If my book was of help, please leave a review on Amazon, even if it's just a sentence or two. It would mean the world to me.

Jayson

Write book take-aways on this page.

www.ingramcontent.com/pod-product-compliance
Lightning Source LLC
Chambersburg PA
CBHW080619190526
45169CB00009B/3237